PINE

Also by Julia Koets

Hold Like Owls

The Rib Joint: A Memoir in Essays

Pine

Julia Koets

Winner of the 2019 Michael Waters Poetry Prize

Southern
Indiana
Review
Press

Published by the University of Southern Indiana
Evansville, Indiana

ISBN 978-1-930508-49-1   First Edition

Printed in the USA

Library of Congress Control Number: 2020943326

This publication is made possible by the support of the Indiana Arts Commission, the National Endowment for the Arts, the University of Southern Indiana College of Liberal Arts, the USI English Department, the USI Foundation, and the USI Society for Arts & Humanities.

Southern Indiana Review Press
Orr Center #2009
University of Southern Indiana
8600 University Boulevard
Evansville, Indiana 47712

sir.press@usi.edu
usi.edu/sir
Ron Mitchell and Marcus Wicker, eds.

Cover art: Images from the Biodiversity Heritage Library. Contributed by Smithsonian Libraries and Missouri Botanical Garden, Peter H. Raven Library.
Cover design: Zach Weigand
Layout: Darrian Breedlove

For all the girls who've lain down in fields

"It is interesting to note in landscape architecture they use the term 'desire lines' to describe unofficial paths, those marks left on the ground that show everyday comings and goings, where people deviate from the paths they are supposed to follow. Deviation leaves its own marks on the ground, which can help generate alternative lines, which cross the ground in unexpected ways."

–Sara Ahmed,

Queer Phenomenology

CONTENTS

"We may never touch queerness, but we can feel it as the warm illumination of a horizon imbued with potentiality [...] we must dream and enact new and better pleasures, other ways of being in the world, and ultimately new worlds."

–José Esteban Muñoz,
Cruising Utopia: The Then and There of Queer Futurity

potentiality

THE SCIENCE OF _____

"The French, I believe, have agreed on the term 'aviation' in case they ever succeed in flying."

−*The Century Magazine*, October 1891

Let's agree on a word for _____ in case
we ever succeed in _____ing. To the girls
who lie down in fields, their bicycles
on their sides, too, like horses
asleep in the sun, know this: even though
_____ is not a science yet, it will be.

When you button your shirt in the morning,
fingers fumbling to fasten the circles,
to thread them through, know that we invented
the word for this science from *bud*, as if
a row of tender orchids will soon bloom
down your chest, a new branch of botany.

Science of radio, science of sleep,
science of kindness, science of the wheel.
One day we will study _____ like we study
flight or photography. Let's agree
on this: everything exists on a spectrum,
word derived from *specter*, science of startle,
science of the remarkable. Two girls
in a field test the science of buttons.
Their shirts soon to break into yellow blooms.

THE BREAKERS

That summer hundreds of moon jellies
    wash up on shore, soft bodies
scintillating at our feet. When we swim

past the breakers, no one on the beach
    can hear us. Sea bells, our diaphragms
swell & let go. Cirrus clouds slide smooth
    as razors across that throat of sky.

As hair on fire, tentacles brush your back.
    Your skin welts pink. The shore
iridescent with moons. The ocean breathes &
    we swim against the pull of its lungs.

EROS AS OXYGEN MASK

: after the EROS (Emergency Respiratory Oxygen System) Crew Oxygen Mask

In a brown paper bag, I test my lungs' capacity
      for fear. No, I test my lungs' capacity for recognizing
it as such. I'm not dying, I tell myself.

      Beside you in bed—my dress on the floor,
your bra next to it—I watch the paper fill
        & diminish, fill & diminish.

      Fear of certain kinds of desire
can manifest in the body like hypoxia.
      A tendency to ignore our feelings
or act on them only in secret—both a kind
      of flight—can result in what a pilot feels
under rapid decompression. Arterial
      constriction, neurologic shock.

The first time I kissed a girl the pressure
      dropped for what felt like hours, my breath short,
my body shaking beside her in bed.

      It's not that I don't want to kiss you. I do.
      It's not that I regret kissing you. I don't.

The altitude in your room reaches 12,000
      30,000   50,000 feet,
as if we're under water or miles above it.
      Could we pass this paper bag—a kind of kiss—
back & forth between us?

IF DESIRE IS ALWAYS A DESIRE
FOR RECOGNITION

"When Hegel made the claim that desire is always a desire for recognition [he was telling us] that to persist in one's own being is only possible on the condition that we are engaged in receiving and offering recognition."

–Judith Butler, *Undoing Gender*

your legs : the pines at the edge

of the marsh : your arms : the boys

fishing from the bridge : your doubt : cedar

shake house : your earlobes : the sink's

slow drips : your patience : the deck

of a ship : the secret we keep : a net

late at night : our flashlights : your mouth

on my skin : the moon through the shells

of the ghost crabs we catch : our skin

nearly translucent : our desire : the tide

line : the tiger shark's teeth we find there

EROS AS FISH

"Eros, who jumped into the Euphrates..."

—Encyclopedia of Astronomy and Astrophysics

"...life in that room seemed to be occurring beneath the sea."

–James Baldwin, *Giovanni's Room*

Seagulls circled our boat, longing.
We cast our lines. We waited for a bite.

Then Jesus took the loaves, offered thanks, and gave
to those who were seated as much as they wanted.
He did the same with Eros.

There was no one to tell us
when the ocean would begin.

All summer we lived in a bowl of glass.
We fastened a rope around our waists
so we would not lose each other.

Look in the sky and you will see us there.
Look in the water—there, too.

BOYS

There were boys whose time I wasted. I didn't know it
at the time. Boy who drove a black car fast, boy who

wore a rubber band around one wrist, across-a-river
boy, boy I kissed underwater. I kept some boys too long,

like sand dollars, starfish. Boy who painted his bedroom floor,
boy who fixed motorcycles, boy who loved the girl I loved,

chrysanthemum-tattoo-on-his-back boy, boy like a shell
I took home to put to my ear to hear *home*, put to my mouth

to call myself there. Boy who wore a watch to bed,
boy who cooked spaghetti, sauce spilled down his shirt,

cheese-toast-in-the-oven boy, yard-strewn-with-yellow-leaves
boy, beach-so-dark-we-couldn't-find-the-path-back boy.

THE BOATHOUSE

On the bottom of Lake Lanier, leaves
      settle. *It's deep enough off the boathouse*
roof, he says. I don't have to fear my feet

might touch the cold, mucky layer of peat.
      Myths of breeding balls of cottonmouths
make me reluctant to jump. He plunges, leaving

me standing barefoot up there. I ease
      toward the edge, watch him hoist himself out
onto the dock, estimate how many feet

lie between me and the surface, how deep
      the water goes. Later, wrapped in towels,
drying off in the sun before I leave,

I try to tell him what I can't easily
      tell him, what seems impossible in the South:
I love a girl. Saying the words, a feat

in itself. When the sun begins to seep
      out of the sky, I drive back to town,
his mother's horse in their field granting me leave.
      Blue Ridge, red river, morning at my feet.

SOLSTICE

On the year's longest day, you decide to float,
      mimic driftwood until the moon catches up
with the sun, a midsummer devotion.

You pull a deflated raft from the shed to blow
      back to life. The long, gold sections scallop
like the shell Venus rode in on. Afloat,

you let one of your feet hang over.
      In between chapters of my book, I covet
the thin ties of your bathing suit. In devotion

to the sun at the end of June, you close
      your eyes. Until the wind picks up,
the water looks flat. The humidity floats,

clings to our skin, a midsummer's cloak.
      If I could measure our fear in cups,
I could fill every pool in town. I devote

the day to this: to try to keep my eyes open
      and stare directly at the sun. Squinting shut,
my eyes halo for a second and snow floats.
      I shiver with so much devotion.

BEACH TOWN ELEGY

If I try to dig to China, anywhere
but where I grew up, water fills the space,

follows me the more I leave. My mother
taught me how to build houses over my feet,

to pack sand over my toes, the dorsal sides,
to ease my heels back, focus on the ground

when I pulled my feet out and houses appeared
in their place. In summer, we map the days

by how far things wash up, the empty sound
of waves dropping teeth on the shore.

BULLFROG DRAWL

You write a poem that fits on your palm
so you won't forget there are things
we invent when we're alone. On balmy

mornings we realize it might have taken all
night for a snail to leave its shimmering
trail across the sidewalk. With my palm

I want to measure the length of its crawl,
weight of its slowness, time for retracting
into its shell. Magnolia and pine embalm

us right before the bottom falls
out. The dogs hunker down and pull, jingling
their collar tags—coats heavy, and paws

all mud. Summer afternoons: rain, then calm—
the ponds so flat they turn to glass, mirroring
our arms, our chests. On particularly balmy

nights, our shirts stick to our skin. The drawl
of bullfrogs in the neighbor's pond is lulling
us to bed. Tonight's line on your palm:
I measure every Grief I meet. And every balm?

EROS AS HIGH SCHOOL

: after Eros High School, Jackson Parish, Louisiana

Dissect a frog's heart in preparation
for losing yours. Memorize "Annabel
Lee." Write an algebraic proof to testify
to how desire is true in every case.
Recite a sonnet. For her. Call it a theorem.

PINE

1. to want without seeing. *"We look before and after, / And pine for what is not."*

2. (archaic) painful desire. *"Long have I dwelt forgotten here / in pining."*

3. tree with needles instead of leaves (loblolly, lacebark, sugar, stone). *"Between every two pine trees there is a door."*

4. (archaic) to torment, to afflict with pain. *"They prick us and they pine us."*

5. what is holy in certain small towns in the South. *"Sacra Pinus Esto: Let the Pine be Sacred."*

6. to suffer with Eros. *"Be still, sad heart! and cease repining."*

7. a hamlet. *"The Pines, a mile-long slice on a 36-mile-long barrier island east of Manhattan along the Long Island coast, was a sanctuary for up to 10,000 gay men during weekends."*

8. pagan symbol of fertility. *"[Pine cones], the sexual organs of the trees, remained green even in the middle of winter."*

9. a kind of medicine, a cure. *"In Paris, France, in the year 1889, a Congress of Physicians, specialists in the field of respiratory disorders, named Summerville, South Carolina, as one of the two places on the face of the earth best suited for the treatment and cure of pulmonary disease [due to the town's curative pine vapors]."*

10. a box for burying. *"Should she get the pine box or a plain white shroud?"*

11. to wilt with loss. *"She too, sad mother! for Ulysses lost Pin'd out her bloom."*

12. to suffer grief. *"Those who throw nets on the water will pine away."*

EROS AS BICYCLE

: after Audre Lorde and the Bianchi Eros

In time, girls who bicycle through their childhoods—
through parks named after flowers that only grow

in hot places, through pet store parking lots,
through churchyards, through every fenced-off place—

begin to associate the wind, entire
and merciful on their skin, with love.

Years later, I drive a back road through a stretch
of swamp, the trees holding us in place.

In time, I look over at the woman beside me
in this landscape, the wind all over my face.

HULL & HOLLOW

We wonder from the road if what's left
    of a boat is worth the drag & pull. Tilted
hull, belly-up with abandon. Bereft

of open water or sail, its stern lies thickset
    with barnacles, algae. Fiddler crabs pilfer
pluff mud, scutter sideways across what's left

of this boat run aground. With heavy
    waves against the starboard, the ocean jilts
the schooner farther from the tideline. Bereft

of cutting through deep water, slick & deft
    in surf, the boat practices stagnancy, wilted
in the marsh. The hull's spine—what's left

of it—slumps from run-ins with oyster beds,
    gnarled tree stumps, seafloor off-kilter
with sandbar and rock. Abandoned, bereft,

desolate out here. This *Dolores*,
    name faint on her stern, left like roadkill
along the two-lane road we drive. Left
    to hull & hollow, belly-up, bereft.

FIELD NOTES ON LOVING A GIRL IN SECRET

There's a danger in comparing her to things.
      Her prayer, a stall of horses. Her anger,
the beak of a bird. Her sleep, a sun-bleached fence.
      Her sadness, a yard pile of firewood.

A patch of pines is all I remember of a field.
      Quiet, she says. Her stick-shift sedan,
her trouble with mathematics, her car radio
      turned up all the way. I write her questions

on a sheet of paper so no one can hear.
      Late at night in my blue car, we drive
back roads, the only place we speak openly.
      The field's full enough tonight, I think,
to break into a thousand wings.

THANK-YOU NOTE TO COLLEGE ALGEBRA

Because arithmetic allows certain formulations, I chose the seat behind X, girl with acrylic nails, girl with pastors for parents, girl with two last names, girl I'd love exponentially. We both tested into the class for our inability to remember the quadratic equation. Square root of landline telephones, square root of knocking-on-doors-to-find-each-other, square root of every-back-road-we-drove. Measuring the lack of floor space in her room, I once tried to figure out how she found any of her clothes. We graphed formulas for the midterm on my top bunk. I know now that if we'd set each factor equal to zero, we'd have solved everything.

EROS AS RECLINER

: after Havertys' Eros

Technically ours wasn't a recliner,
but an oversized synthetic leather
tilt-back chair. Regardless, don't lean into
easy conclusions about the metaphor.
Neither of us was lazy about love
and we hardly ever watched TV. Yes,
we slept some Saturdays past noon. *Most*
Saturdays is more accurate. But we enjoyed
certain inaccuracies. The 2.3 spoons of milk
we poured to make macaroni and cheese
from the box. The unevenness after
we trimmed each other's hair on the kitchen
stool late into the night. The jeans
we cut to shorts right off each other's legs.

When we leaned back in that chair together,
I could hear the thick spring at the center
bending under us. I wonder, if I'd known
what to listen for, if I might have heard
the sound of her desire bending, too.
She, who insisted on being straight,
on her inclination for that lazy boy
who hung out in our room all semester.
Not knowing what we were in for, she and I
leaned into it, overcome.

APPLE SEASON

There's something primordial about knees,
        she tells me. Not nervous system or heart
but joint, hinge, seam. We leave our small city,

drive several hours north to Upcountry.
        The trees are beginning to end, to start
the falling season. Last week my knees

turned red, skin raw on the rough upholstery
        of her couch. She kissed me smart,
put her hand under my skirt. In a city

so small and southern, I worried our bodies
        might set off an alarm, a flare in the dark
open field behind her place. Was it Nie-

tzsche who said, at least once it's necessary
        to doubt all things? Or was it Descartes?
These nights, we doubt our parents, the cities

of Sodom and Gomorrah, Adam and Eve,
        the churches we grew up inside. We harvest
bushels of apples, get down on our knees,
        pick up ones that fell like burning cities.

SOLSTICE

We stay up later and later that fall.
We wait for the longest night. We shine

a flashlight into the field behind your place
and see at least twenty eyes staring back,

like ships at night. I've every intention to run
until you grab my hand. *Deer,* you say.

They're more afraid of us.
Are we on a sea or in a field

so open we can see our latency—
field of doubt, field of apprehension,

sea of potentiality. The deer stay
until all we hear is wind in their place.

AUGUST

You read my poems like prayers said
        over breakfast. The field out back rusts
shut for half an hour as the sun sits up in bed.

Summer mornings as a girl, my head
        still dizzy with sleep, my mother shuttled
us to the neighborhood pool. I hardly said

a word that early, the light just a thread.
        I was always the last one in, eating breakfast
cross-legged on the concrete edge. The bed

of grass along the chain-link fence sheeted
        with dew. A couplet I show you: *In August /
our hair turns green with penitence.* A priest said

prayer begins at the temple, the forehead,
        the way the water hit me when I trusted
my head first into the pool. Diving into that bed

of water, I woke up, my arms treading
        darkness like prayer, my eyes slowly adjusting
to see. One morning over breakfast, you said
        a good poem is like that: a kind of bed.

ELEGY FOR SELENOGRAPHY

Maria, not oceans as Galileo
    first thought. We align our telescope
with Mare Nectaris, saccharine so sweet
    the moon's sick with it. Maria, not fullness,

but want. You time your affection so no one suspects
    we're more than friends. *Magnificent
desolation*, Buzz Aldrin said of the moon's landscape.
    One night I dare you to skinny-dip with me,

no one in sight. In the best of worlds,
    which isn't our world, I imagine
how we dive into Mare Cognitum,
    sea where all becomes known.

DAUGHTER ELEGY

When I want to know what our biological children
    would look like, you say,
                    It's impossible.

You're right, in the literal sense, but you aren't normally
    so precise.
                    Imagine a girl, I tell you.
I'd keep a tally on our fridge, make a science
    out of how many books you both read each week, month, year.

We'd cook squash blossoms on her birthday,
                    fill them with the best ricotta.
    One night I'd tell her
                    how I helped you dye your hair
one summer, how I covered your shoulders
    with an old blue towel, how I couldn't
comprehend how
                    something so purple—
nearly cosmic,
    reminiscent
                    of a nebula in deep space—
    could turn
                    your hair
    the shade of harvest moon.

MOON WEDDING

Girls drop moon rocks
down the aisle we walk.

We call them basalt girls,
gabbro girls, norite girls.

Our parents here no more
than the man on the moon.

Rings around our fingers,
Jupiter's gossamer bands.

We wear pale blue spacesuits,
like two robin's eggs speckled

with lunar dust. No one can hear
our vows when we speak them.

EROS AS BUS

: after Eros Bus Travel, Reus, Spain

Our particular story involves a bus
        the shade of liquid amoxicillin.
The hostel walls, too,   like a mouth

      with bright light inside.   She has a boyfriend,
                  so I reason   when she goes to kiss me:
        I loved her first,   *before.*

      She says, *Let's put the mattress on the floor,*
                  afraid   the hostel walls are pink azalea
        petal thin.   She doesn't want anyone hearing

she's anything but straight.   Tomorrow night
                an overnight bus so pink it will be impossible
    to sleep
will take us from Corfu to a ferry to Athens.

                I'll wonder as the pink strobes
light up the aisle: how far in advance

could I see it coming: falling for her again   like a fact
      up ahead in the road   an animal   crossing in the dark.

"The stock-in-trade of the gay and lesbian archive is ephemera, the term used by archivists and librarians to describe occasional publications and paper documents, material objects, and items that fall into the miscellaneous category when being cataloged."

—Ann Cvetkovich,
An Archive of Feeling: Trauma, Sexuality, and Lesbian Public Cultures

ephemera

SHED

1. an antler that's fallen off the head of a deer, elk, or moose. *Searching for a shed in the woods is a study in loss.*

2. to take off one's clothing. *We shed our clothes all over your floor.*

3. to lose (hair, leaves, feathers, skin) naturally. *I shed my hair all over your bathroom floor.*

4. to spill. *We shed our clothes like milk on your floor.*

5. of tears or blood. *"Hot were the tears Achilles shed for Patroclus."*

6. (archaic) of a river, to overflow its banks. *A river can shed itself into the sea, but then it is impossible to separate the river from the sea.* (See: watershed 1] a drainage basin; 2] a point of transition between two conditions. *Define the watershed between friendship and desire.*)

7. a structure built for shelter. *We kiss secretly in the shed in your parents' backyard.*

8. a hiding place. *Can we live inside a poem (the line: a floorboard; metaphor: a nail; the page: a shed)?*

9. a fragment. *This poem is only part of the story, a shed of the story.*

10. to resist being affected by. *Know that we invented* shed *from* shade, *as if to draw the blinds in a room.*

11. to cleave, to divide something with a knife. *When dissecting a heart, shed delicately.*

12. (archaic) to put out a fire. *Our bodies are a fire we cannot shed.*

ANTLERY

: after an old photograph on my wall

A picture of us hangs like a rack of antlers,
      bone shed & regrown at the pedicle.
(No one can step into the same river

twice, even after twelve years.) A cervid's
      horns grow faster than most bones are able.
The picture of us hangs like a rack of antlers,

deciduous outgrowth, both show & dagger:
      we made each other the loveliest & most awful.
(No one can step into the same river

twice, but we've tried to hold one another
      as we were.) Velvet growths from the skull,
both of wooing & wounding, our antlers

differ in the number of tines: fixtures
      of wanting, of waging war. (How cruel
when we try to step in the same river

again.) In the photograph, your hair's a color
      it is no longer. Each winter the pile
in my yard grows dangerous with antlers.
      I mistake a forest fire for a river.

ALTERNATE NAMES FOR WINTER

: The Dogs Won't Go Outside

: How to Light the Pilot

: I Rarely See Your Thighs

: Steam from the Laundry Room

: Every Song About Trouble

: The Oven Wide-Open

: How the Trees Grow Bones

: How the Pines Stay the Same

ANTLERY

Our want grew, & it makes sense
        that it grew from our heads. *Sex is mostly*
mental, you said. But, really, I sensed,

we were out of our heads, off-balance,
        out of line: the cost of loving secretly.
We tricked ourselves (foolish innocence)

into thinking we could want without consequence.
        If I compare desire with deer: quietly
through snow at night, finding the scent

of every buried thing. In its defense
        (I'm always defending desire), maybe
it's what we needed to get through. I sense

this is the very logic of want. The sequence
        of events that got us here arguably
follows this thought: you came to my senses.

Put another way: I couldn't make sense
        of myself until you showed up. You and me,
two girls in the South, didn't make sense.
        Fear made us biblical, animal, unsensed.

LOVE IN AN EFFICIENCY APARTMENT

A gust of wind reasons with our window.
        Tiny sugar ants binge on anything
they can carry up the wall. Stories below,
        city buses lurch. The wires they hold
spark like lighthouses breaking down.

The bed we bought off Craigslist
        leaves our hips sore most mornings.
In a bowl by the sink plums ripen
        around their stubborn pits. The cat
paws a cockroach, a playful twitch
        in her small, sharp mouth.

Morning leans against our bedroom wall:
        the sky, a field of rusted stars,
or thousands of those lighthouses, signaling.

ANTLERY

Our antlers differ in the number of tines,
      slender points sharp enough to keep us
safe. You always loved a good fight,

an extension of the skull, a barbed bite.
      We survived on bitterness, bulb of amaryllis.
Our antlers differ in the number of tines

that came back from the coronet, site
      of all of our breaking. I mistook trust
for an acre of bones. A good fighter

finds which trees will sharpen tines to spikes;
      picks words that most resemble cusps,
keen points of a broken moon. Our tines

grow skyward as the rows of pines
      lining the interstate. Two girls in love.
We both knew too well that a good fight

starts at the ankle, moves itself up by
      way of the knee, the hip, throat, rust
tint of your hair. Our antlers differ in tines
      each time we return from a fight.

EROS AS OPERATING SYSTEM

: after EROS (Extremely Reliable Operating System)

When I compile a Google document
of every online communication
between the two of us over eight years—

the peacocks in your parents' yard.
the smallest church in the South—

I realize how reliable desire
seemed—*house lit so brightly it hurt to look—*

even when we operated with troubled
assumptions about it: your persistence

on a single narrative of queerness,
story in which you didn't consider
yourself a character. *Are you asleep?*

I worry sometimes, though, that damage
is a system more reliable than desire.
A Facebook message you sent included
an attachment from my hometown paper:

Wife jailed after stabbing husband
with ceramic squirrel. I laughed, of course,
but we came close to breaking
the skin. *National Forest*

in the Tenderloin. chiropractor sign
made from real back bones.

ANTLERY

: *after measuring the sky*

Antlers depend on the length of daylight
      & how well you're taking care in the woods.
Are you keeping your mind on the height

of trees, the coarseness of grass, the blight
      of certain red cedars & brier? You should.
Antlers depend on the length of daylight,

so don't spend too many hours inside. The mind
      tends to wander itself to wormwood
if you don't keep occupied with the height

of sky, that fence at the clearing's edge, right
      where the mountains start, that pile of firewood.
Antlers depend on the length of daylight,

how long the sun's glare stays in your sights.
      Notice each year how the strawberry bush
comes back. Stay occupied with the slight height

of dandelions, purslane, the muscadine
      that fits your mouth like a good word.
Antlers depend on the length of daylight.
      I keep my mind on the sun's height.

ONE THEORY OF LOSS

accounts for horses on the moon. Droves
of lunar shires gallop across the dusty surface:

equine, opaline, sibylline. Two thousand pounds
weightless, theoretical without atmosphere.

The mane at the crest of each horse's neck
reveals how we're taught to hold tightly

to each others' bodies. We don't know how
we could ever let go. To understand

this theory of loss, we must train ourselves
to think like astrophysicists, to recognize

the greatest disproved improbability here:
this species learned to breathe without air.

A SURE BREAK

The apples come like bruises; the horses
      never sleep in the stables. From my bedroom window
I put myself to sleep by counting their tall, coarse

bodies awake in the field. In my dreams, our divorce
      is measured as a trainer determines the growing
height of steeds: from the withers of the horse,

right between the shoulder blades. I'm not sure
      how to decipher the dream, our letting go.
I only know my mind keeps running that course,

an animal awake in the field every night. The store
      of tension down my neck and spine: a row
of autumn fruit ready for a horse's

mouth, the sure break of skin. Every morning,
      the horses are just as I left them in the narrow
hours. Still tired, I wake to the sun coursing

through my rented room. The giant sycamore
      at the far corner of the field loses its shadow
as the sun keeps coming. At the fence, the horses
      wait, brown faces like a row of apple cores.

EROS AS EYEGLASSES

: after St. Moritz's Eros

"Put your finger here; see my hands.
Reach out your hand and put it into my side."

—John 20:27

My father an optometrist, my mother
a photographer, I'm mindful of sight.

I noticed you when I first saw you.
I paid close attention to your eyes.

Since your father's a pastor and your mother's
a pastor, were you born with a propensity

for vision, too? We were earnest in our view
of god, of who we could and couldn't see,

the confession, a kind of tonometry.
My family's cat scaled the picket fence

blind, her eyes glaucomic, glassed-over.
Her thighs, torso, jowls, and shoulders

risked the jump to that spiked height,
her field of vision a field of nothing

but faith. One night I sunk my teeth gently
into your side, just enough to see.

TEACHING ON CHINESE NEW YEAR

Two third graders ask what year I was born.
　　They flip through a book of animals
that symbolize each year, each birth. *The boar,*

they say. *"According to the Jade Emperor,*
　　you were twelfth, last. At the river, you ambled
too long. You're intuitive, but jealous, born

sensitive and seeking beauty." I want more,
　　What else does it say? They point to bristles,
tusks, hooves. When a sow's young aren't yet boars,

she's most dangerous if surprised or cornered.
　　"You're indecisive," they add. It's only cruel
in its certainty. *How old are you? Were you born,*

one of them asks, *when my mother was born?*
　　I've never celebrated Chinese New Year until
this year, year of the rabbit. Like the boar,

the rabbit's prone to holding onto memories
　　until their palms are sore, and the river's full
of stones. It snowed in March when I was born
　　two weeks late. My mother bore and bore.

NIGHTJAR, OPENING

I'm sorry for the birds. The stanzas brimmed
with wings, of species whose names utter:

*yellowthroat, red-throated loon, white-throated
needletail, ruby-throated hummingbird.* Scale-

throated measure, bare-throated caesura,
scan the distance between *nesting* and *wintering*,

thin space distinguishing *call* from *song*,
signaling *boundary* from *attracting a mate*,

the sound of a nightjar opening its beak
like a lid, tightly-sealed, to *sing*.

OVERGROWTH

A woman's saying *help* behind our house
      tonight, her voice hard to make out at first.
Can you hear it, I ask, *what's that sound?*

Her voice so low you feel it, a ruffed grouse
      thumping its wings in the dark. We're not sure
how far away or close she is to the house.

The lights in the surrounding yards are out,
      and the moon's not any help. The thirst
in her voice dries my throat. No other sound,

no one else, her voice appears unannounced—
      we wonder who's there, who's after her.
I call the police, give the address to our house.

Tall and sure in the dark, an officer shouts
      to another near the cars. Their flashlights search
the overgrowth for what caused the sound.

Have I misheard the night, the wind in its mouth?
      We lie awake in bed, not sure if they discovered
her. The police drive off. Behind our house
      it's still. *I can't sleep,* I say without a sound.

A LOVE POEM TO SALLY RIDE

I want to tell you something about the inside
of a horse. Not the guts or the organs,

but the way a current can travel
through skin like wind through a field.

When I say *field*, I know
you're already thinking of gravity,

the gravitational field
surrounding a body like the skin

around an apple. A horse notices
the rough calluses on my palm

when I hold an Elstar out to him.
When I say *body*, Sally, I know

my associations are too earthly. Remind me
that one day on Mercury lasts one hundred

and seventy-six days on Earth. Let's go back
to the Carrington solar flare of 1859,

a solar wind, the telegraph operator's fingers
shocked in the middle of a sentence.

A live electric fence around a field
of beautiful horses sent a pulse

through my hands and down my arms
when I was ten years old and grasped

the wires to get a closer look at them.
I knew something then about fear, what it takes

to keep what's inside in. I didn't know
exactly how a horse would react

to such a shock, but I hypothesized,
the way an astronomer determines

a black hole exists: by measuring
the electromagnetic radiation

experienced by a surrounding star.
Sally, Tam said you never openly told

your mother, your dad, or your sister, Bear,
that the two of you were a couple,

partners for twenty-seven years.
She said you met when you were twelve.

If wormholes really existed, I'd go back
to when the nerves inside your body glowed

electric with fear; I'd tell that twelve-year-old you
that this year James Obergefell took Ohio to court

when the state refused to recognize *marriage*
on his husband's death certificate. One week

before you died, Tam told you she worried
people wouldn't know who she was when you

were gone, the sinews between the two of you
cut like wire, leaving a hole big enough

for a horse to slip through. *Don't be afraid,*
I'd tell you. Last month when the case went

to the Supreme Court, the ruling legalized
same-sex marriage. People are changing, Sally,

the way comets aren't constant objects, but
celestial happenings, always in flux.

When you flew to the moon, you gave me
a lunar amulet—not pearl or locket, but satellite.

Sally, I'd give you a coterie of moons.

THANK-YOU NOTE TO *E.T.'S* ELLIOTT

There are boys biking across the moon tonight. The forest is sure of it. I turn on the kitchen sink as hot as it will go. Steam cloaks the window. Thank you for waiting so late into the night, for falling asleep in that lawn chair at the end of my girlhood. For years, the glow of the tool shed was the only thing.

Your brother and sister and mother and your dog are asleep inside and your father is in Mexico. You taught me how to stand on a boy's back and kiss the prettiest girl I know. The floor, covered in frogs.

I leave a handful of Reese's Pieces in all the places she and I used to go: Yesterday's Tavern, the concrete-slab porch of my first apartment, the flimsy futon from my college dorm room. At the grocery store check-out in our old neighborhood I drop a few orange pieces in the "extra pennies" dish.

I toss a baseball through a doorway and expect it to come back. I buy a pot of dead flowers and wait for them to bloom. The tips of my fingers mimic the moon.

A VILLANELLE FOR JODIE FOSTER

In *Contact*, you wait for sound. Radio
        static in deep space keeps you awake
long into the night. *How small this globe,*

Ellie Arroway thinks. Miniscule, close
        to insignificant. It'll likely take
lifetimes to hear the farthest star, radio

frequencies scientists debate. History's slow,
        the way some satellites in space
appear to stand still, orbiting the globe.

Small moves, small moves, your father's canto.
        They should've sent a poet, you say,
witness to another galaxy. Without radio

proof, no one believes what you saw. *No
        future,* they say, *is quite so opaque.*
When you come out at the Golden Globes,

your silver dress glittering, all the stars aglow
        in the audience, you speak about privacy,
but also wish, in your own brave voice, a radio
        wave, *to be not so very lonely* on this globe.

MOON PRAYER

Tonight the moon lies on its back:
a thin, white spine. I count each vertebra
of the woman next to me in bed,
map her lumbar curvature:

each bone : a moon : a linear diagram
down her back. In this parable
in which I am an astronomer
the night sky is a body capable of holding
what may not survive our atmosphere.

Oh god of well-made darkness,
let us not forget how prayers have been cruel,
how the moon has been misconstrued
for a knife glinting in the dark.

WELCOME GIFT

Our friends move into the house with the oak
     growing out of the deck and find *Patience*
& Sarah, a used book, in their mailbox. No note,

no clue to who left it. On the cover: two women
     reaching for each other under a row of pines.
They aren't quite touching, as if summoned

for a portrait they're hesitant to take, a stance
     we all know well. We're good at reluctance,
never holding hands in public or dancing

at weddings. This welcome to their street
     as clear as the water in the harbor:
they can't see what brushes over their feet.

When the neighbor's moonflower-white cat
     wanders into their yard after dinner—
a gleam in the grass—they can't help but ask,

is this, too, a welcome? The wisteria wrapping
     every tree like a gift, the screech of shoes,
boys shooting hoops at the end of the cul-de-sac—
     this, too? This, too?

PRESERVATION

The only things remaining are things we kept
  in jars. The house smelled like library books &
coming home to a person. We hardly slept

& didn't seem to need it. We were adept
  at disorder. Stacked books could barely stand
beside the bed. What remains: things we kept

nailing to the walls: city map where traffic leapt
  in the streets; photograph of your father—a candid
shot. He's young, thin. We hardly slept

in summer months when winged things crept
  in the windows. Or woke us with their landing,
stunned taps against the glass. Things we kept

lined our windowsills: jar measuring the depth
  of rainfall that year, jar holding a handful
of stones we rubbed soft. We hardly slept

but woke whole afternoons: your face, windswept,
  out of order; the ocean lapping up the sand.
The only things remaining are things we kept
  coming home to. Place where memory slept.

EROS AS ASTEROID

"The following observations of Eros were made with the 40-cm. (Clark), equatorial
telescope of the Washburn Observatory."

−G.C. Comstock, "Observations of Eros," 1901

When I look at love through a telescope,
I see Psyche, Eros's largest crater,
three miles across. You remember the story:

the most beautiful daughter, Venus's jealousy,
an arrow's mistake, the lover who only appears
at night and never shows their face, an oil burn,
Persephone's beauty in a box.

I draw sky charts by hand to find you.
I look for you in every darkness.
I make the following observations of Eros:
bruises, the marks your fingers left on my thighs,
look like the sky at the end of the night.

VERNAL EQUINOX

Talk's small and laundry hangs on string
      across the kitchen. Morning light, like woald,
dyes your hair and our walls with its rising.

You hum threads of songs while ironing
      a shirt. Forgiveness has been thin, a camisole.
The back door's held open with string

so our orange cat can spend the morning
      on the stoop. I crack four eggs on a bowl's
thin rim; the yolks intact, each rising
like a brass button in the glair.

                  Then you're mending
a tear in my jeans and one in the shoulder
of your favorite shirt.
            Imagine heat as string:
with steam, you fix my chiffon dress, threading
water through each wrinkle.
                Like a thousand pressed stoles,
the sky's clean: new cloth, taut and rising.

Breakfast almost ready, the eggs sizzling
in the pan.
            The sun's just a pinhole,
the wind, a needle closing up a seam. Clouds rising
and so threadbare I can hear the snapping strings.

NOTES

"Eros as fish"

Lines are taken and modified from John 6:11: "Jesus then took the loaves, gave thanks, and distributed to those who were seated as much as they wanted. He did the same with the fish." A line is borrowed and altered from Adrienne Rich's poem "Diving into the Wreck": "there is no one / to tell me when the ocean / will begin."

"Bullfrog Drawl"

Line taken from Emily Dickinson's poem "I measure every Grief I meet."

"Pine"

Each definition uses a quotation from a source:

1. "We look before and after, / And pine for what is not" is from Percy Shelley's poem "To a Skylark."

2. "Long have I dwelt forgotten here / in pining" is from Anne Brontë's 1837 poem "A Voice from the Dungeon."

3. "Between every two pine trees there is a door" is from a quotation John Muir wrote on his copy of Emerson's *Prose Works*, Volume 1.

4. "They prick us and they pine us" is from Sir Walter Scott's 1855 novel *The Bride of Lammermoor*.

5. "*Sacra Pinus Esto* (Let the Pine be Sacred)" is the motto of my hometown, Summerville, South Carolina.

6. "Be still, sad heart! and cease repining" is from Longfellow's poem "The Rainy Day."

7. "The Pines, a mile-long slice on a 36-mile-long barrier island east of Manhattan along the Long Island coast, was a sanctuary for up to 10,000 gay men during weekends" is taken from Chloe Coleman's June 30, 2017, *Washington Post* article titled "'It was one tiny bit of the world that was ours.' Polaroids of the men of Fire Island Pines."

8. "[Pine cones], the sexual organs of the trees, remained green even in the middle of winter" is from Gary M. Devore's 2008 book *Walking Tours of Ancient Rome: A Secular Guidebook to the Eternal City*.

9. "In Paris, France, in the year 1889, a Congress of Physicians, specialists in the field of respiratory disorders, named Summerville, South Carolina, as one of the two places on the face of the earth best suited for the treatment and cure of pulmonary

disease [due to the town's curative pine vapors]" is from *Porch Rocker Recollections*, a book my mother and her friends wrote in 1980 about the town where I grew up.

[10.] "Should she get the pine box or a plain white shroud?" is from Michael Chabon's *The Yiddish Policemen's Union*.

[11.] "She too, sad mother! for Ulysses lost *Pin'd* out her bloom" is from Book XV of Homer's *The Odyssey*.

[12.] "Those who throw nets on the water will pine away" is from Isaiah 19:8.

"Eros as bicycle"

Based on lines from Audre Lorde's poem "Visit to a City Out of Time": "In time / people who live / by rivers / dream / they are immortal."

"Shed"

"Hot were the tears Achilles shed for Patroclus" is from Homer's *The Iliad*.

"Antlery (A picture of us hangs like a rack of antlers)"

Lines based on Heraclitus's quotation: "No man ever steps in the same river twice, for it's not the same river and he's not the same man."

"Eros as operating system"

This poem references a December 2013 news story from *The Post and Courier*.

"A Villanelle for Jodie Foster"

This poem references the 1997 science fiction film *Contact* and when Jodie Foster came out publicly for the first time in her acceptance speech at the 2013 Golden Globes Awards ceremony. She ends her speech by saying, "Jodie Foster was here, I still am, and I want to be seen, to be understood deeply, and to not be so very lonely."

ACKNOWLEDGMENTS

I'm grateful to the editors of the following journals where some of these poems first appeared, sometimes in different forms or under different titles.

The Carolina Quarterly: "Bullfrog Drawl" and "Field Notes on Loving a Girl in Secret"

Connotation Press: An Online Artifact: "The Boathouse," "Eros as fish," "A Love Poem to Sally Ride," "Solstice (We stay up later and later that fall)," and "A Sure Break"

Fall Lines: "Apple Season," "Boys," "Elegy for Selenography," "Eros as bus," and "Eros as oxygen mask"

The Frank Martin Review: "Love in an Efficiency Apartment," "Overgrowth," and "Welcome Gift"

The Minnesota Review: "Preservation"

Miracle Monocle: "Moon Prayer," "Moon Wedding," and "One Theory of Loss"

Nimrod: "Vernal Equinox"

Portland Review: "Eros as recliner"

Qu: "The Science of _____"

Southern Indiana Review: "Alternate Names for Winter," "Eros as asteroid," and "A Villanelle for Jodie Foster"

I would also like to thank the Ohio Arts Council for the 2018 Individual Excellence Award and the South Carolina Academy of Authors for the McCray Nickens Fellowship.

Thank you to Ron Mitchell for your enthusiasm and support of this project. To Michael Waters and Marcus Wicker for believing in this book.

I am grateful to my mentors and friends at the University of Cincinnati who read drafts of this project and so many of my villanelles in workshop. You all helped me make this book better: John Drury, Danielle Deulen, Rebecca Lindenberg, Jim Cummins,

Sara Watson, Dan Groves, Linwood Rumney, Michael Peterson, Lisa Summe, Rochelle Hurt, Sarah Rose Nordgren, Emily Skaja, Lisa Ampleman, Madeleine Wattenberg, Caitlin Doyle, and José Araguz. Thank you to Christine Mok for teaching courses on performativity and for introducing me to the work of Sara Ahmed, José Esteban Muñoz, and Ann Cvetkovich. To Amy Chuch, Hannah Godwin, and Anne Wright. To Jillian Weise, Jenny Johnson, Meg Day, John Drury, and Michael Waters for taking the time to write your generous words about the book. To Kelly Blewett, Anne Valente, and Carla Sarr for your friendship during the writing of this book. My thanks and love to Jacqui Simmons Groves for reading multiple drafts of this book and for your endless support.

Thank you to my family and friends for their love. To Lindsey, Dolores, and Tiny. These poems would not be here without you.

Photo by Eleanor Brownlee Koets

Julia Koets is the winner of the 2017 Red Hen Press Nonfiction Book Award judged by Mark Doty for *The Rib Joint: A Memoir in Essays*. Her first poetry collection, *Hold Like Owls* (University of South Carolina Press), won the 2011 South Carolina Poetry Book Prize judged by National Book Award winner Nikky Finney. Koets's essays and poems have recently appeared in *Creative Nonfiction*, *Indiana Review*, *The Los Angeles Review*, and *Portland Review*. She has an MFA in creative writing from the University of South Carolina and a PhD in literature and creative writing from the University of Cincinnati. Koets is an assistant professor of creative nonfiction at the University of South Florida.

www.juliakoets.com

The Michael Waters Poetry Prize was established in 2013 to honor Michael's contributions to *Southern Indiana Review* and American arts and letters.

MWPP Winners

2019—Julia Koets

2018—Chelsea Wagenaar

2017—Marty McConnell

2016—Ruth Awad

2015—Annie Kim

2014—Dennis Hinrichsen & Hannah Faith Notess

2013—Doug Ramspeck